Hug a Teddy

and 172 other ways to stay safe and secure

BY JIM ERSKINE AND GEORGE MORAN

FREDERICK MULLER LIMITED
LONDON

First published in Great Britain in 1981 by
Frederick Muller Limited, London NW2 6LE

Text copyright © 1980 by James R. Erskine
Illustrations copyright © 1980 by George Moran

All rights reserved. No part of this book may be reproduced or utilized in any form or by any means, electronic or mechanical, including photocopying, recording, or by any information storage and retrieval system, without permission in writing from Frederick Muller Limited.

Printed in the United States of America
DESIGNED BY BETTY BINNS

ISBN: 0 584 10765 X

**To Sharon, Frog, and Mr. Boldman,
survivors all.**

J. E.

It is folly to bolt a door with a boiled carrot.
—ENGLISH PROVERB

Boil everything.

Keep smelling salts handy.

Make a will.

Staple your hat on.

Watch your blood pressure.

Take vitamins.

Peel the fruit.

Avoid strange infants.

Hang a quarantine sign on the front door.

Dream nice dreams.

Run from cows.

Don't answer the telephone.

Buy presents for your boss.

Make friends with the police.

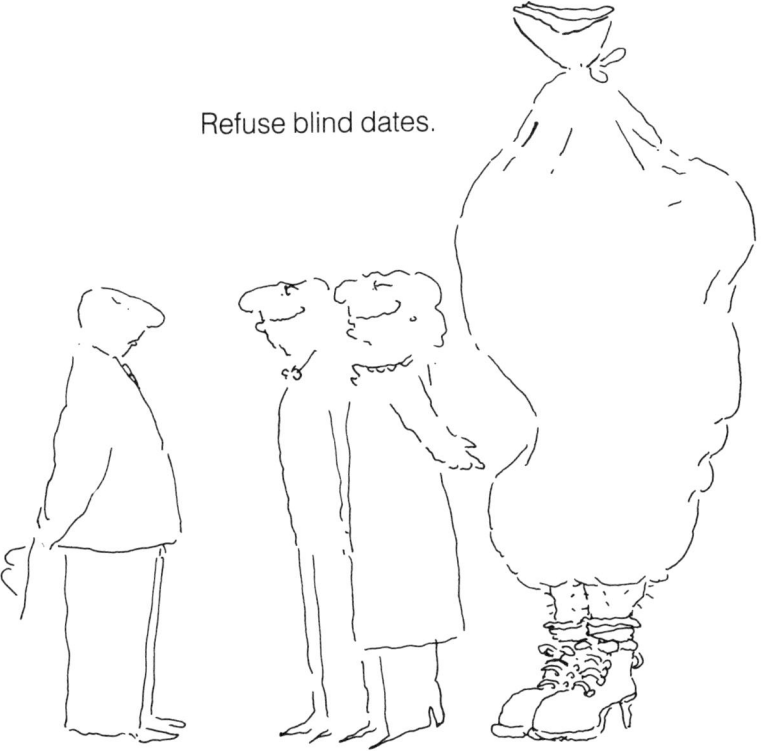

Carry spares.

Run from responsibility.

Say "Nice doggie."

Sew name tags on all your clothes.

Call your mother every Sunday.

Sit facing the door.

Mountain climb mole hills.

Don't lend anyone your toothbrush.

Memorize *Wanted* posters.

Keep your hand out of the pickle jar.

Sleep in a crib.

Don't swallow your chewing gum.

Clean your ears.

Keep your finger out of the
pencil sharpener.

Wear armor.

Put windshield wipers on your eyeglasses.

Wear your boy scout uniform.

Check out the fire exits.

Don't sign anything.

Nail everything to the floor.

Arrange an alibi.

Inspect your gums.

Jog.

Hide.

Buy a German shepherd.

Wear a gas mask.

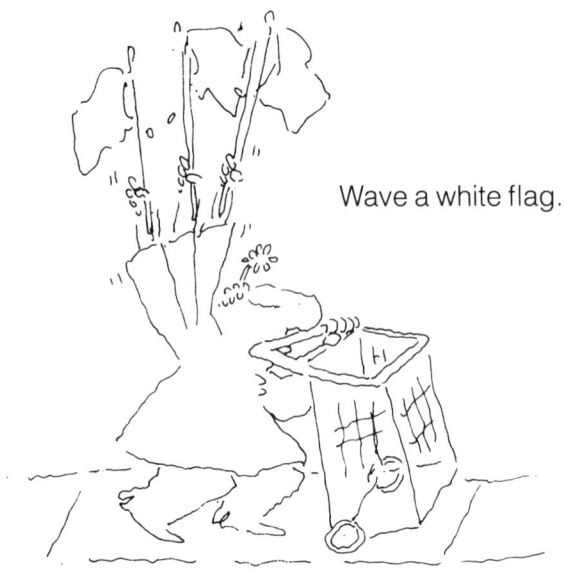

Wave a white flag.

Carry your money in a sock.

Prepare for burglars.

Always carry an umbrella.

Make the dog taste-test your food.

Sterilize your socks.

Hire a bodyguard.

Ask for a third opinion.

Learn karate.

Practice first aid.

Ski on a flat surface.

Wear colors that glow in the dark.

Never lick more than three books
of trading stamps at one time.

Avoid gamma rays.

Use an alias.

Wear cleats.

Always bring your booties.

Marry money.

Clip the cactus.

Run away.

Remember your algebra,
just in case.

Chew everything
32 times.

Fight by proxy.

Take a flashlight wherever you go.

Leave fresh cookies for Santa.

Pay your bills on time.

Pass up the creamed zucchini.

Reserve a hospital room.

Give snakes the right-of-way.

Shun evil.

Make yourself the beneficiary
of your life insurance.

Shower nine times a day.

Carry a map.

Wear suspenders *and* a belt.

Keep your glass in a safe place.

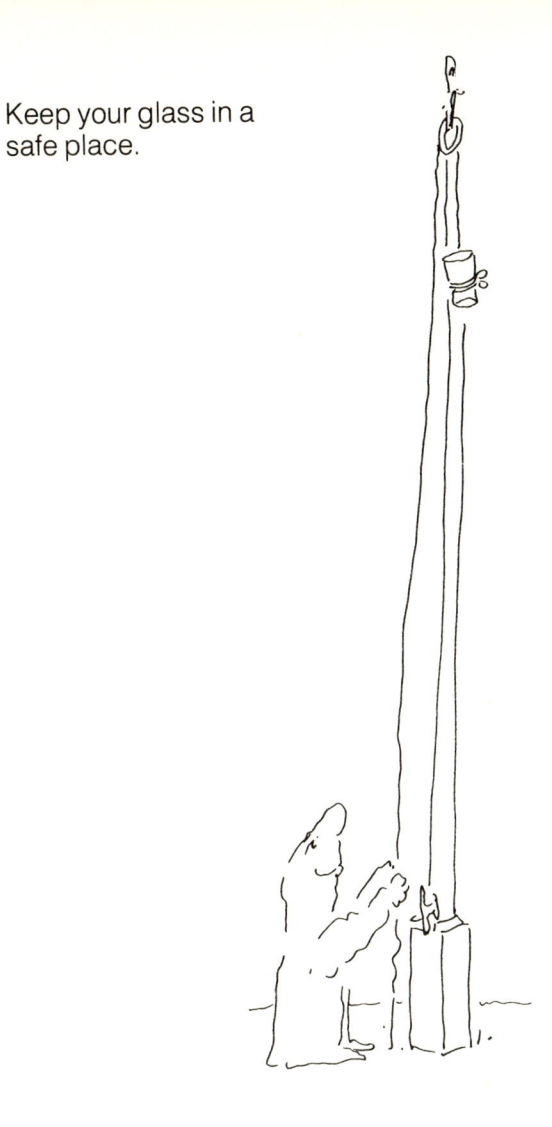

Wear the right size pants.

Soak packages in the tub.

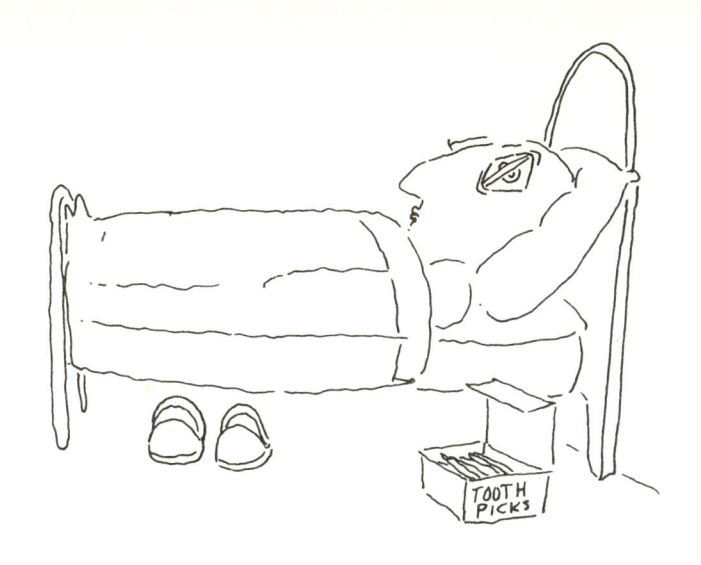

Sleep with one eye open.

Count your change.

Hug a teddy.

Breathe.

HAK!
HAK!
HAK!

Shave your peach.

Install seat belts on the rocking chair.

Don't cheat.

If you do, don't get caught.

Don't peek into a cannon.

Leave your mail unopened.

Wait your turn.

Think positive.

Put training wheels on your bicycle.

Always carry
your passport.

Talk sweetly.

Trust no one.

Don't body surf on escalators.

Voice your opinion
where no one can hear you.

Read the fine print.

Memorize the penal code.

Keep your night light on.

Hire a double.

Agree with anybody bigger than you are.

Never grant interviews.

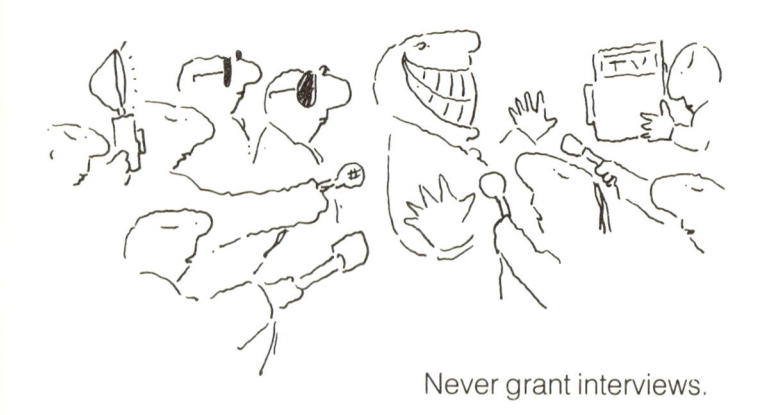

Write your diary in secret code.

Launder your money.

THIKA
THIKA
THIKA

Floss.

Don't kiss on the mouth.

Remember your anniversary.

Don't dance on the roof.

Pray.

Take no chances.

Never trust birds.

Don't get sunburned.

Wear water wings in the bathtub.

Watch only Shirley Temple movies.

Travel in pairs.

Be nice to your mother-in-law.

Carry rabbits' feet.

Never step on cracks.

Plead for mercy.

Hold your nose.

Dig a moat.

Bar the windows.

Stay away from anyone named HONEST JOHN.

Change your phone number every month.

Lock your doors.

Prepare for an alien invasion.

Ask to see the chef first.

Buy soft furniture.

Read directions carefully.

Provide your own silverware.

Be on time.

Brush your teeth constantly.

Eat veggies.

Study self-help books.

Talk about your problems.

Love yourself.

Mind your own business.

Smoke chocolate cigarettes.

Avoid romantic entanglements.

Play possum.

Wear a parachute in the elevator.

Cover everything with plastic.

Disguise your voice on the phone.

Refuse challenges to duel.

Disinfect your lover.

Declaw the canary.

Sleep a lot.

Hang on to the airplane.

Never cross the street.

Wear long underwear.

Roller skate on the sidewalk.

Never eat in a place called MOM'S.

Live on an island.

Walk around ladders.

Consult a fortune-teller.

Set booby traps.

Register at a hotel as John Smith.

Line your shoes with fur.

Shave with a rubber blade.

Have your newspaper censored.

Fumigate the house.

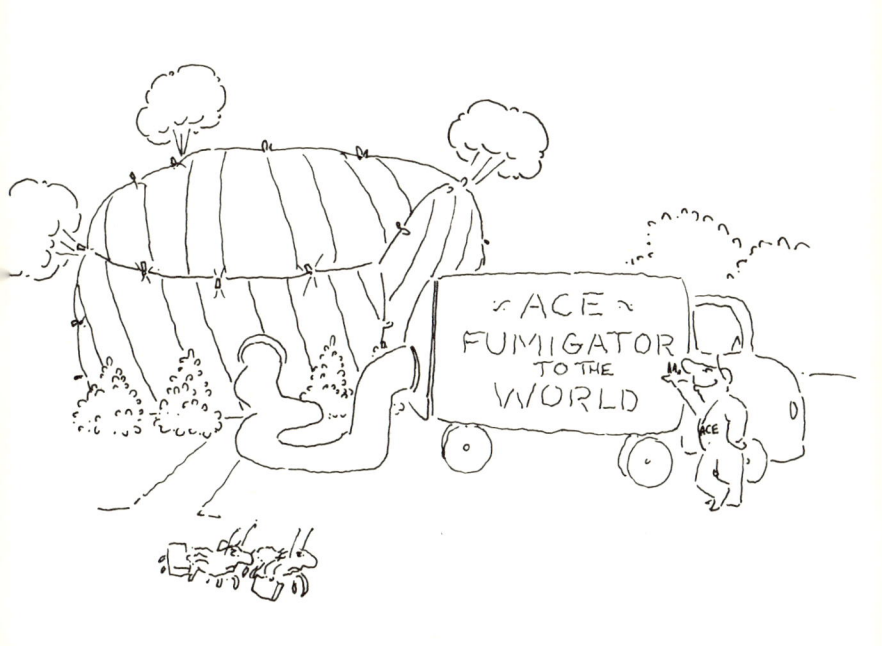

Bury your most treasured possessions.

Write *Do not enter* on all the doors.

Build a fallout shelter.

Live in it.

Play dumb.

Curl up in a ball.

Relax.

Surround yourself with barbed wire.

Avoid quicksand.

Eliminate the opposition.